The (

Cycling Guide

1999/00

*Use this guide with the official route map
available from Sustrans 0117 923 8893*

Gina Farncombe

Curlew Press

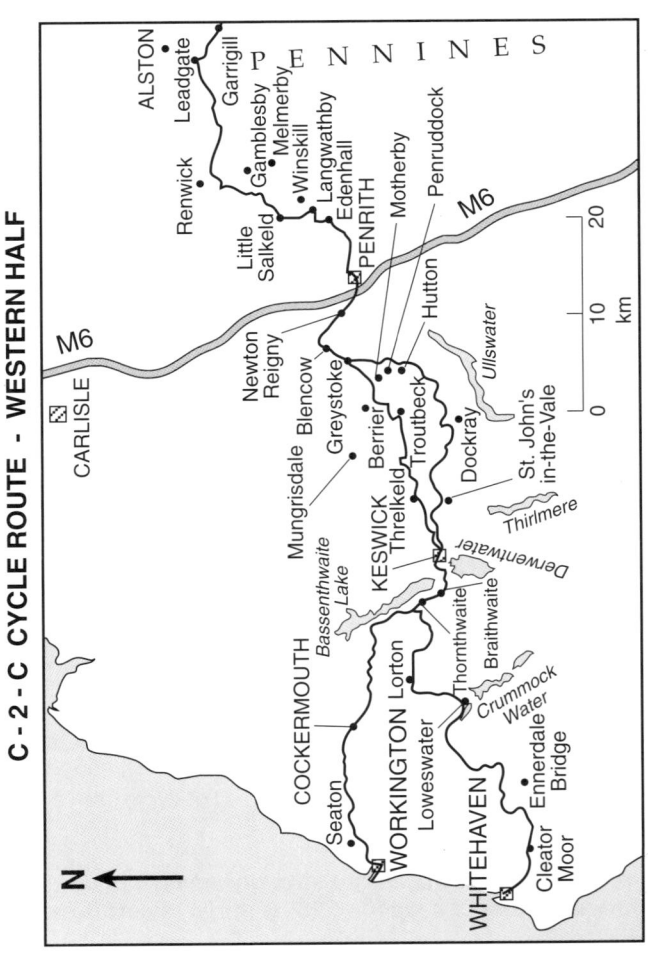

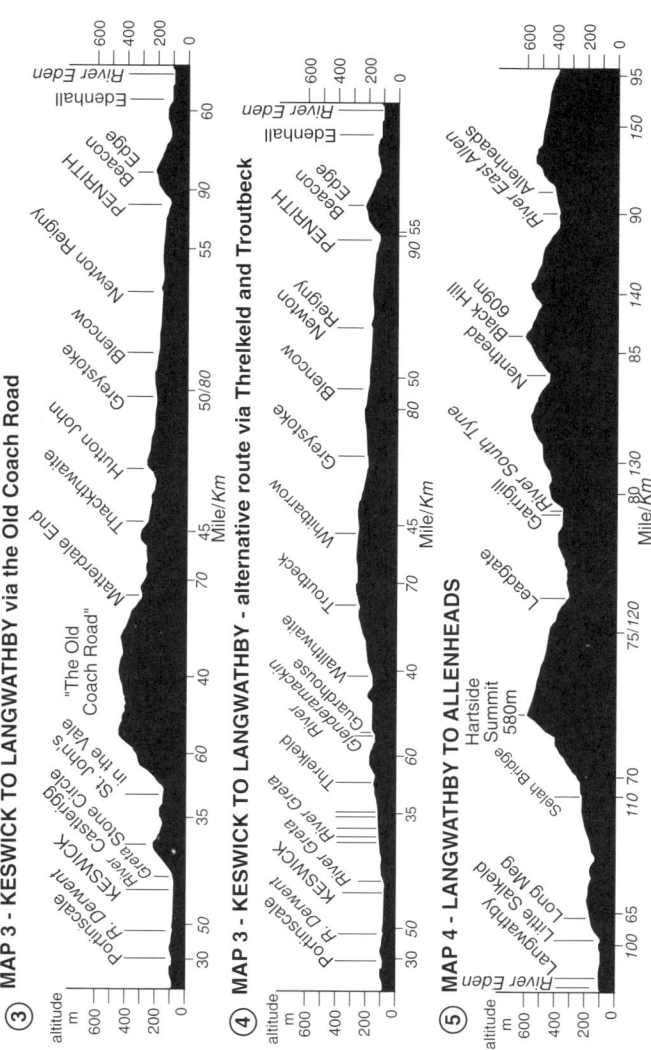

MAP 3 - KESWICK TO LANGWATHBY via the Old Coach Road

③

altitude
m
600
400
200
0

Portinscale
R. Derwent
KESWICK
River Greta
Castlerigg
St. John's Stone Circle
in the Vale
"The Old Coach Road"
Matterdale End
Thackthwaite
Hutton John
Greystoke
Blencow
Newton Reigny
PENRITH
Beacon Edge
Edenhall
River Eden

30   50   35   40   60   70   45   Mile/Km   50/80   55   60   90

MAP 3 - KESWICK TO LANGWATHBY - alternative route via Threlkeld and Troutbeck

④

altitude
m
600
400
200
0

Portinscale
R. Derwent
KESWICK
River Greta
River Greta
Threlkeld
River Glenderamackin
Guardhouse
Wallthwaite
Troutbeck
Whitbarrow
Greystoke
Blencow
Newton Reigny
PENRITH
Beacon Edge
Edenhall
River Eden

30   50   35   40   60   70   45   Mile/Km   80   50   55   90

MAP 4 - LANGWATHBY TO ALLENHEADS

⑤

altitude
m
600
400
200
0

River Eden
Langwathby
Little Salkeld
Long Meg
Selah Bridge
Hartside Summit 580m
Leadgate
Gargill (River South Tyne)
Nenthead
Black Hill 609m
River East Allen
Allenheads

100   65   110   70   75/120   Mile/Km   80   130   85   140   90   150   95

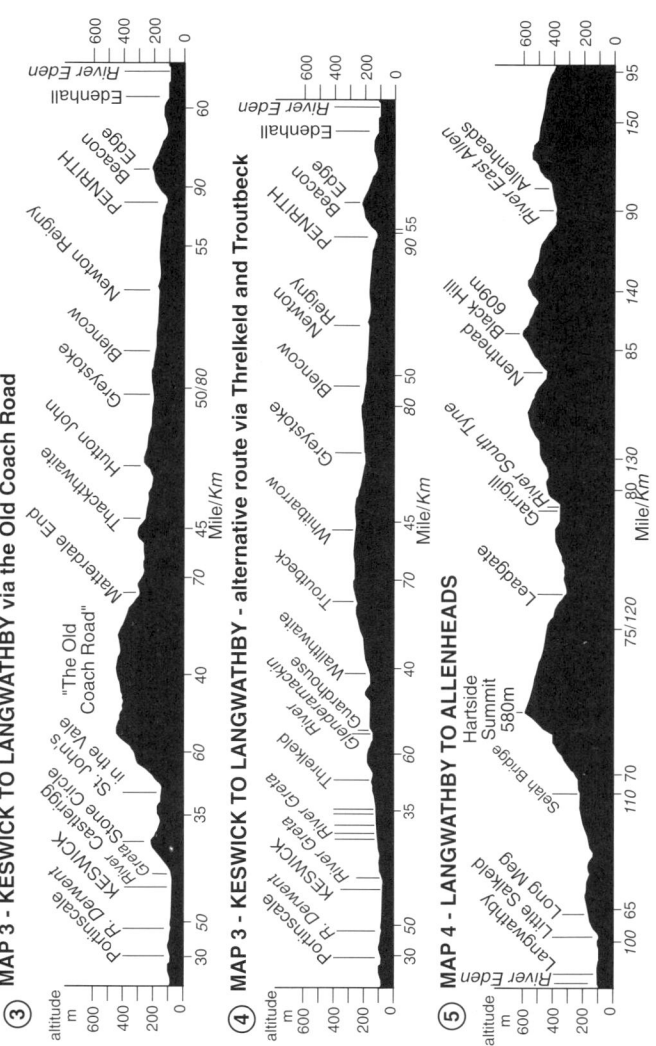

③ MAP 3 - KESWICK TO LANGWATHBY via the Old Coach Road

altitude m — 600 400 200 0

Portinscale · R. Derwent · River Greta · KESWICK · Castlerigg Stone Circle · St. John's in the Vale · "The Old Coach Road" · Matterdale End · Thackthwaite · Hutton John · Greystoke · Blencow · Newton Reigny · PENRITH · Beacon · Beacon Edge · Edenhall · River Eden

Mile/Km scale: 30 · 50 · 35 · 60 · 40 · 65 · 70 · 45/75 · 50/80 · 55 · 90 · 60

④ MAP 3 - KESWICK TO LANGWATHBY - alternative route via Threlkeld and Troutbeck

altitude m — 600 400 200 0

Portinscale · R. Derwent · River Greta · KESWICK · River Greta · Threlkeld · Glenderamackin · River Glenderamackin · Wallthwaite · Guardhouse · Troutbeck · Whitbarrow · Greystoke · Blencow · Newton Reigny · PENRITH · Beacon · Beacon Edge · Edenhall · River Eden

Mile/Km scale: 30 · 50 · 35 · 60 · 40 · 65 · 70 · 45 · 80 · 50 · 55 · 90

⑤ MAP 4 - LANGWATHBY TO ALLENHEADS

altitude m — 600 400 200 0

River Eden · Langwathby · Little Salkeld · Long Meg · Selah Bridge · Hartside Summit 580m · Leadgate · Garrigill · River South Tyne · Nenthead · Black Hill 609m · River East Allen · Allenheads

Mile/Km scale: 95 · 100 · 65 · 105 · 110/70 · 75/120 · 80 · 125 · 130 · 85 · 140 · 90 · 150 · 95

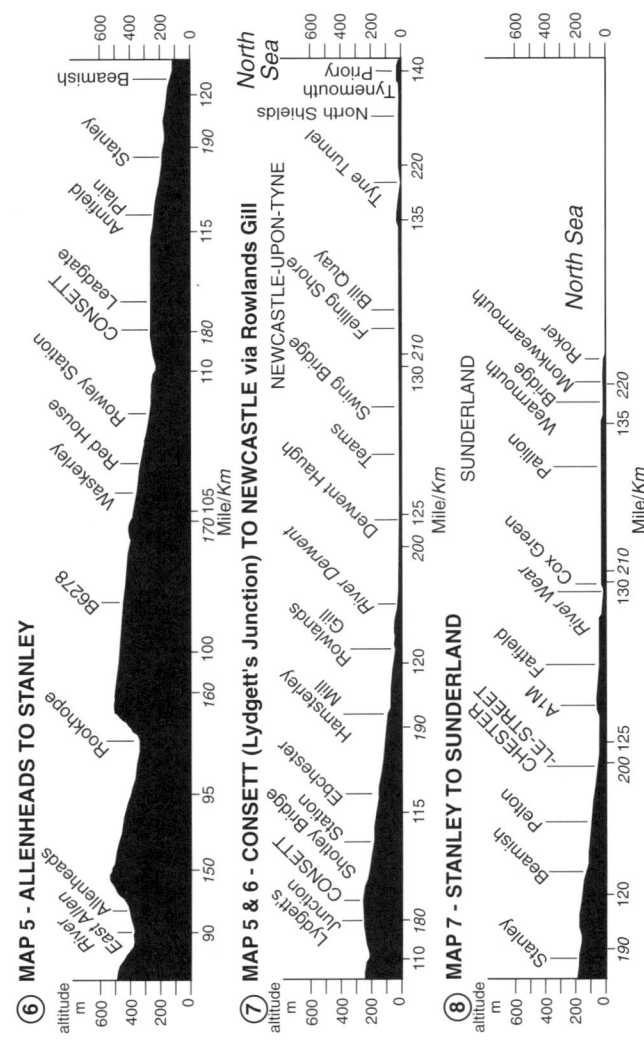

MAP 5 - ALLENHEADS TO STANLEY

altitude m: 600, 400, 200, 0

Beamish — 120
Stanley — 190
Annfield Plain — 115
CONSETT Leadgate — 180
Rowley Station — 110
Red House — 170 105 Mile/Km
Waskerley —
B6278 — 100
Rookhope — 160
East Allen — 95
River Allen — 150
Allenheads — 90

MAP 5 & 6 - CONSETT (Lydgett's Junction) TO NEWCASTLE via Rowlands Gill

North Sea

NEWCASTLE-UPON-TYNE

altitude m: 600, 400, 200, 0

Tynemouth Priory — 140
North Shields —
Tyne Tunnel — 220
Bill Quay — 135
Felling Shore —
Swing Bridge — 130 210
Teams —
Derwent Haugh — 125
River Derwent — 200
Rowlands Gill — 120
Hamsterley Mill — 190
Ebchester — 115
Shotley Bridge —
CONSETT Station — 180
Lydgett's Junction — 110

Mile/Km

MAP 7 - STANLEY TO SUNDERLAND

North Sea

SUNDERLAND

altitude m: 600, 400, 200, 0

Roker —
Monkwearmouth —
Wearmouth Bridge — 220
Pallion — 135
Cox Green —
River Wear — 130 210
A1M Fatfield —
CHESTER-LE-STREET — 200 125
Pelton —
Beamish — 120
Stanley — 190

Mile/Km

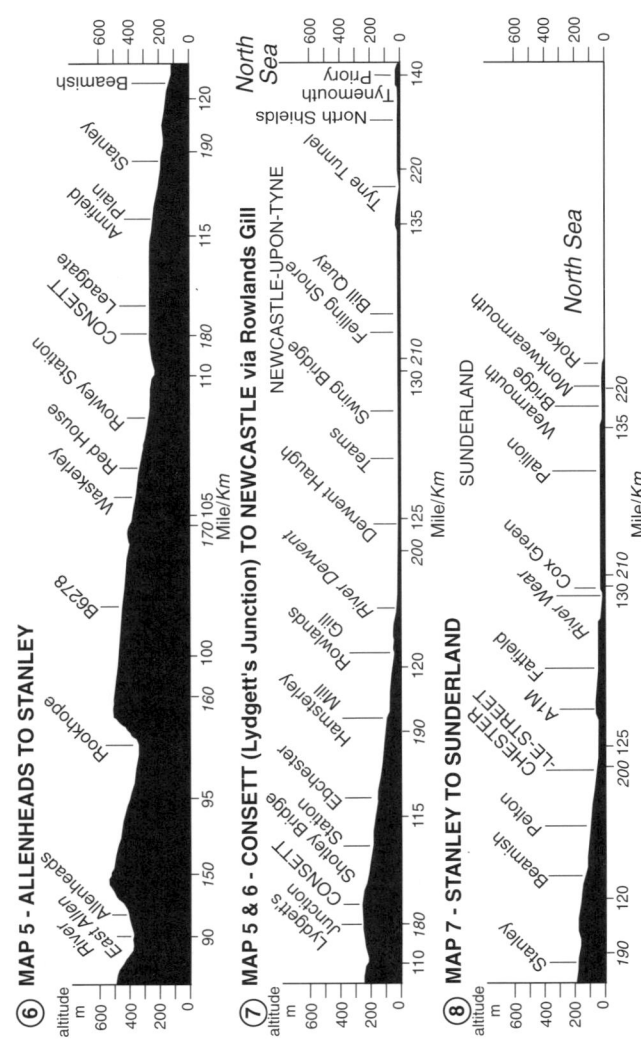

⑥ MAP 5 - ALLENHEADS TO STANLEY

Beamish · Stanley · Annfield Plain · Leadgate · CONSETT · Rowley Station · Red House · Waskerley · B6278 · Rookhope · East Allen · River Allen · Allenheads

600 400 200 0 altitude m

120 190 115 180 110 105 Mile/Km 170 100 160 95 150 90

⑦ MAP 5 & 6 - CONSETT (Lydgett's Junction) TO NEWCASTLE via Rowlands Gill

North Sea · Tynemouth Priory · North Shields · Tyne Tunnel · NEWCASTLE-UPON-TYNE · Bill Quay · Felling Shore · Swing Bridge · Teams · Derwent Haugh · River Derwent · Rowlands Gill · Hamsterley Mill · Ebchester · Shotley Bridge Station · CONSETT · Lydgett's Junction

600 400 200 0 altitude m

140 220 135 130 210 125 200 120 190 115 180 110 Mile/Km

⑧ MAP 7 - STANLEY TO SUNDERLAND

North Sea · Roker · Monkwearmouth · Wearmouth Bridge · SUNDERLAND · Pallion · Cox Green · River Wear · A1M · Fatfield · CHESTER-LE-STREET · Pelton · Beamish · Stanley

600 400 200 0 altitude m

135 220 130 210 200 125 120 190 Mile/Km

C - 2 - C CYCLE ROUTE - WESTERN HALF

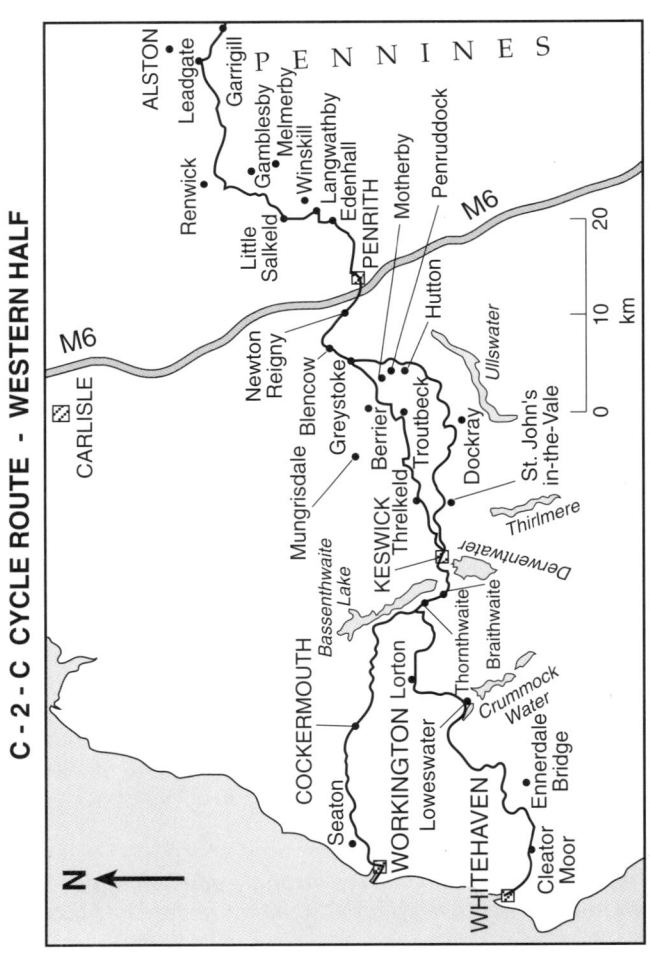

CARLISLE

M6

PENNINES

ALSTON
Leadgate
Garrigill
Renwick
Gamblesby
Melmerby
Winskill
Langwathby
Edenhall
Little
Salkeld
PENRITH
Motherby
Penruddock
Newton
Reigny
Hutton
Greystoke
Blencow
Berrier
Troutbeck
Dockray
Ullswater
Mungrisdale
KESWICK
Threlkeld
St. John's
in-the-Vale
Thirlmere
Bassenthwaite
Lake
Derwentwater
COCKERMOUTH
Lorton
Thornthwaite
Braithwaite
Crummock
Water
Seaton
WORKINGTON
Loweswater
WHITEHAVEN
Ennerdale
Bridge
Cleator
Moor

N

km
0   10   20

6

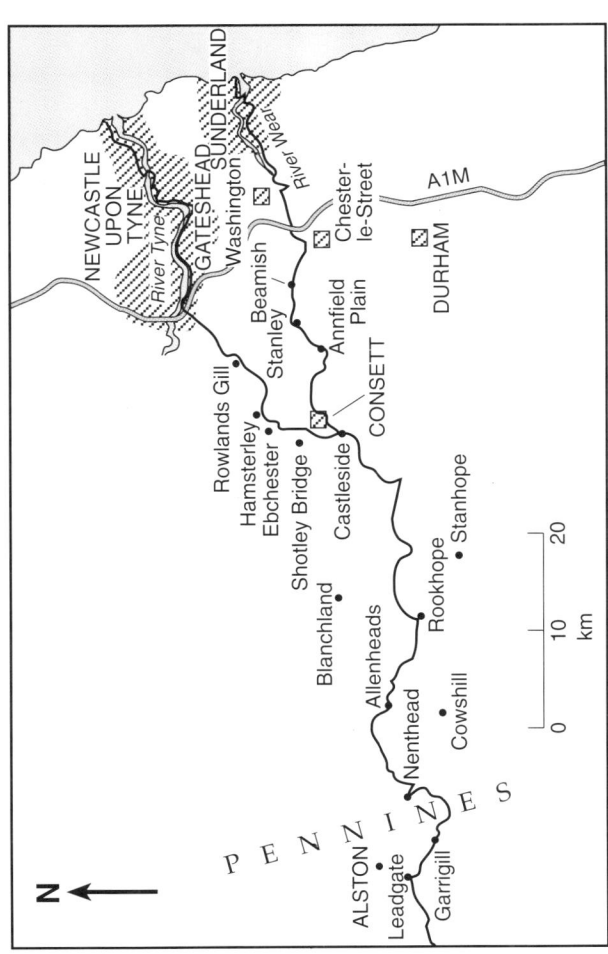

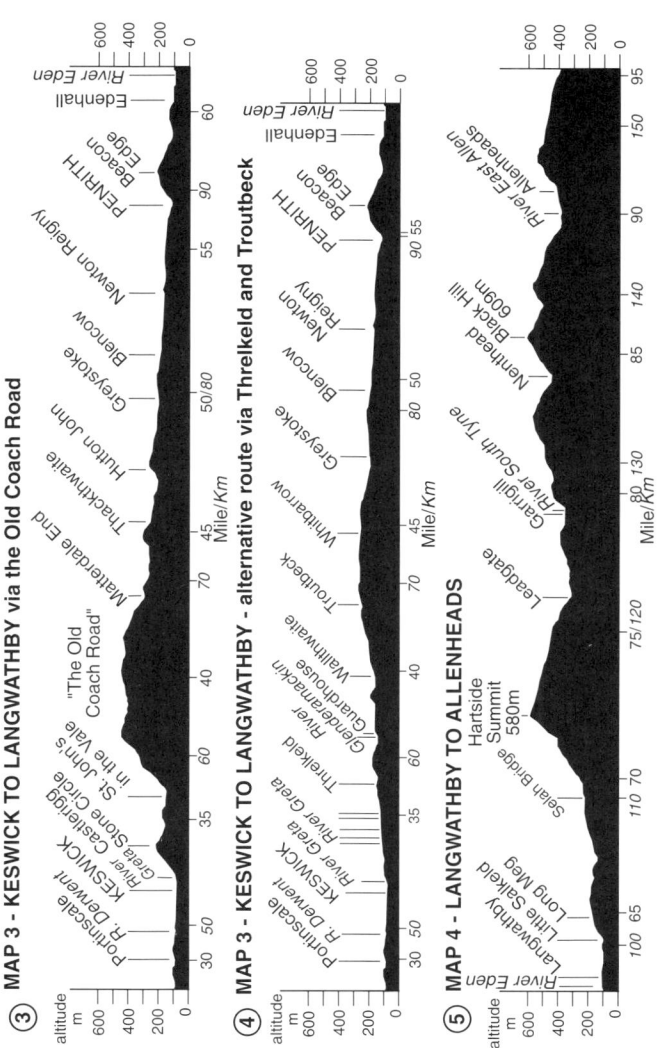

③ **MAP 3 – KESWICK TO LANGWATHBY via the Old Coach Road**

altitude m — 600, 400, 200, 0

River Eden · Edenhall · PENRITH · Beacon Edge · Newton Reigny · Blencow · Greystoke · Hutton John · Thackthwaite · Matterdale End · "The Old Coach Road" · St. John's in the Vale · Castlerigg Stone Circle · River Greta · KESWICK · R. Derwent · Portinscale

Mile/Km: 30/50, 35, 45/70, 50/80, 55, 90, 60

④ **MAP 3 – KESWICK TO LANGWATHBY – alternative route via Threlkeld and Troutbeck**

altitude m — 600, 400, 200, 0

River Eden · Edenhall · PENRITH · Beacon Edge · Newton Reigny · Blencow · Greystoke · Whitbarrow · Troutbeck · Wallthwaite · Guardhouse · River Glenderamackin · Threlkeld · River Greta · KESWICK · R. Derwent · Portinscale

Mile/Km: 30/50, 35, 40, 45, 80, 50, 90 55, 90

⑤ **MAP 4 – LANGWATHBY TO ALLENHEADS**

altitude m — 600, 400, 200, 0

River East Allen · Allenheads · Nenthead Black Hill 609m · Garrigill River South Tyne · Leadgate · Hartside Summit 580m · Selah Bridge · Langwathby · Little Salkeld · Long Meg · River Eden

Mile/Km: 65, 100, 70, 110, 75/120, 80, 130, 85, 140, 90, 150, 95

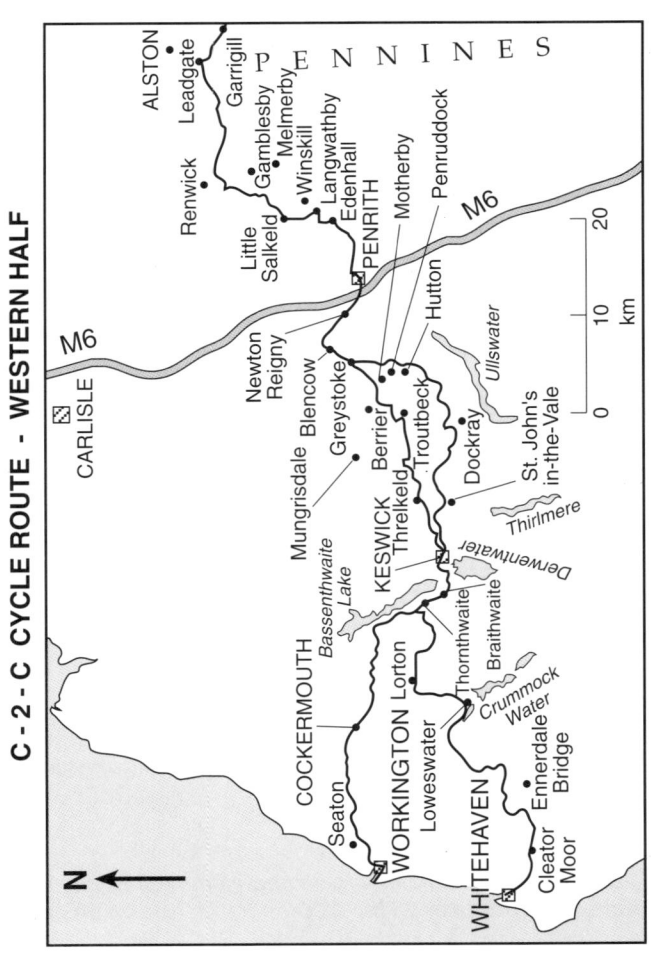

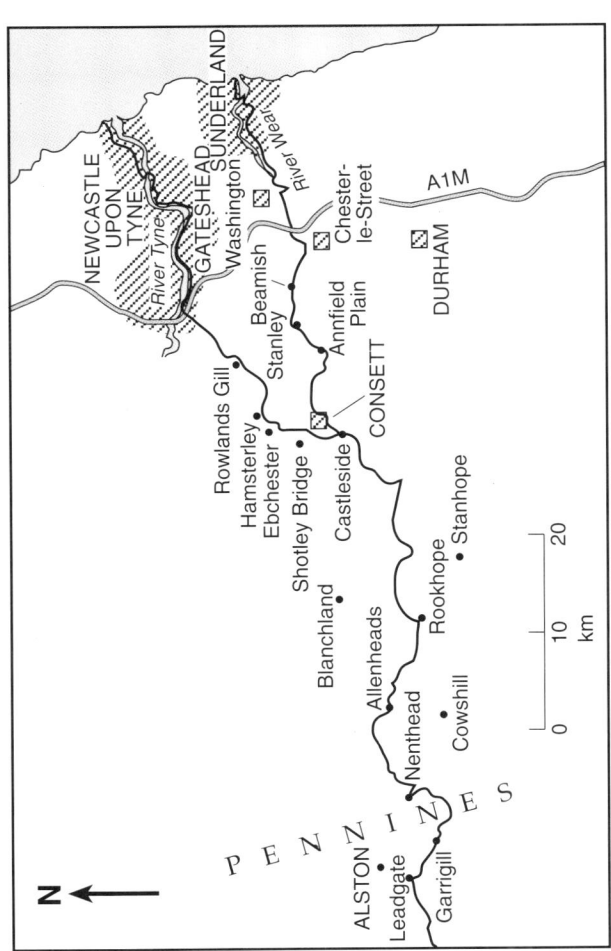

C - 2 - C CYCLE ROUTE - EASTERN HALF

7

The C2C & Reivers B&B Cycling Guide

1999/00

Use this guide with the official route map available from Sustrans 0117 923 8893

Gina Farncombe

Curlew Press

6th Edition	*C2C National Cycle Route*
Edited by	Gina Farncombe
Published by	Curlew Press Croft House Newton Reigny Penrith Cumbria CA11 0AY Tel 01768 863298
e-mail Web page	curlew@croftcot.u-net.com cumbria.com.accom/cycling.htm
	© Curlew Press 1999 ISBN 1 901224 03 1
Distributed by	Cordee Books and Maps 3a de Montfort Street Leicester LE1 7HD Tel 0116 254 3579
Front/back cover	On your bike magazine

Contents

Accommodation place names (west-east)

INTRODUCTION

Welcome to the C2C B&B Guide. This guide is designed to be used with the C2C Sustrans Map obtainable from Sustrans, 35 King Street, Bristol BS1 4DZ, tel. 0117 926 8893.

Your hosts have all been chosen for their understanding of the cyclist's needs, a warm welcome, acceptance of muddy legs, a secure place for your bike and provision of a meal either with them or at a nearby pub. Have a great holiday!

Accommodation is listed from the West to East Coast, not only because the map works this way but also because cyclists benefit from the prevailing wind at their back. If at all possible, please book accommodation, meals and packed lunches in advance, and do not arrive unannounced expecting beds and meals to be available! If you have to cancel a booking, please give the proprietor as much notice as you can so that the accommodation can be re-let.

Your deposit may be forfeited: this is at the discretion of the proprietor.

Suggestions for additional addresses are most welcome, together with your comments.

Please note: the information given in the Guide was correct at the time of printing and was as supplied by the proprietors. No responsibility can be accepted by the Independent B&B Guide as to completeness or accuracy, nor for any loss arising as a result. It is advisable to check the relevant details when booking.

Where do I start the C2C ....?

The best way to cycle the C2C is from West to East coast. If you want to return to the West Coast via the Reivers Route the gradients will be to your advantage.

By Train
To get to Whitehaven or Workington by train you must change on to a local line at CARLISLE. The journey takes about 1 hour,. It follows the coastline and is dramatic and spectacular. Remember, it is essential to book your bike on the train well in advance.

Train enquiries	0345 484 950
Cycle reservations	0345 125 625

Return by Train
From Sunderland, continue to cycle up the coast to the main-line station at Newcastle. Remember, the local train from Sunderland will only take a total of 2 bikes. You will need to make speccial arrangements for more bikes.

By Car
If you have to come by car most landladies will allow you to leave your vehicle with them. There is secure long-term car parking in Whitehaven 'phone the TIC on 01946 592302, or use one of the taxi services on page 100 or cycle back on the Reivers Route!

Note Back-up vehicles are strongly advised to use main roads in order to keep the C2C as traffic free as possible.

C - 2 - C CYCLE ROUTE - WESTERN HALF

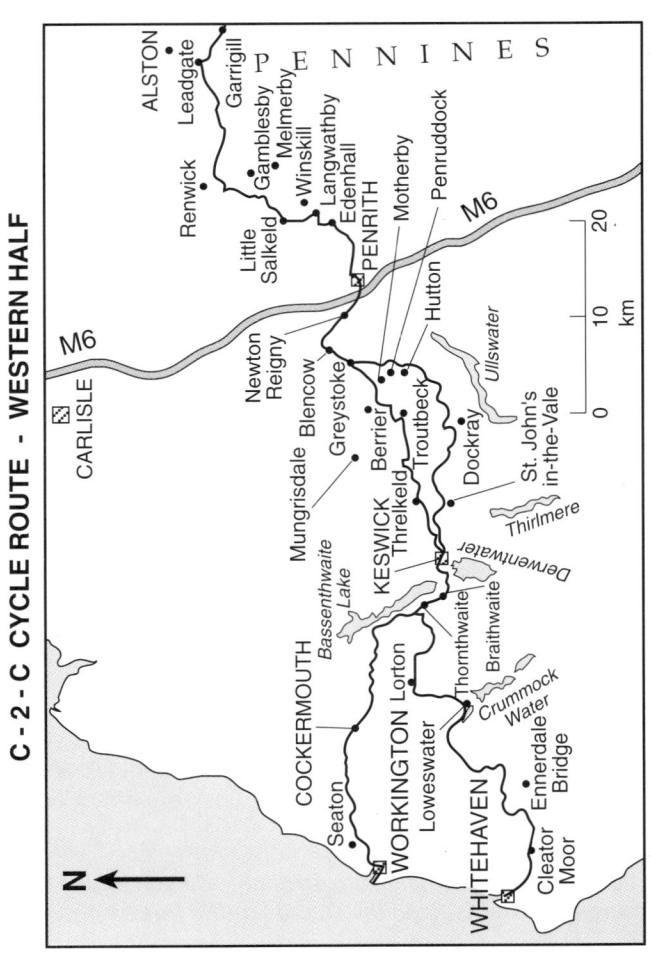

6

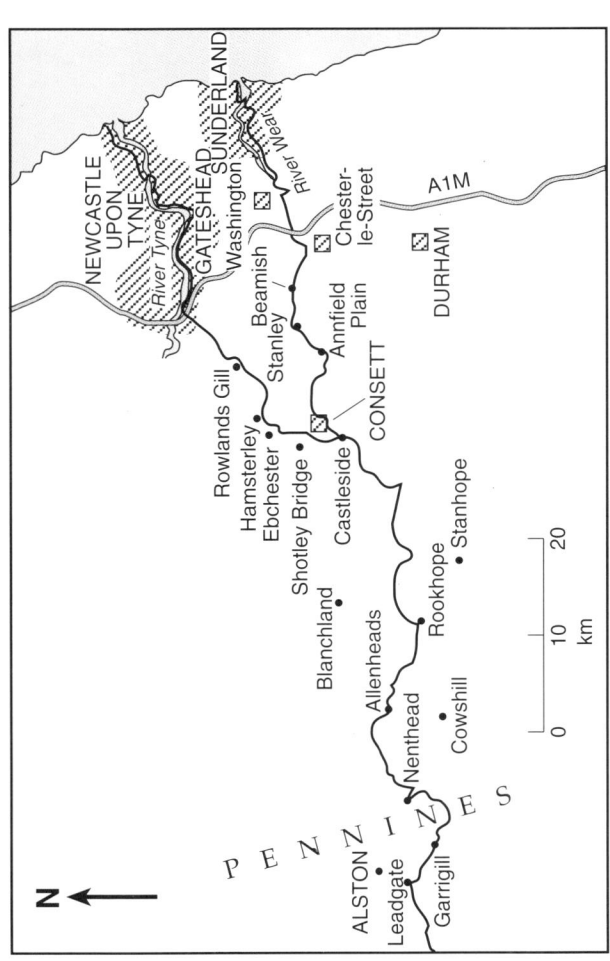

C - 2 - C CYCLE ROUTE - EASTERN HALF

TOPOGRAPHICAL CROSS-SECTIONS OF THE C-2-C CYCLE ROUTE

The C-2-C is 140 miles in length. It is strongly advised to ride the route from West to East, giving the benefit of the prevailing westerly winds at your back. As seen from the topographical sections, the uphill biking is short and sharp, and the downhill biking is long and gentle.

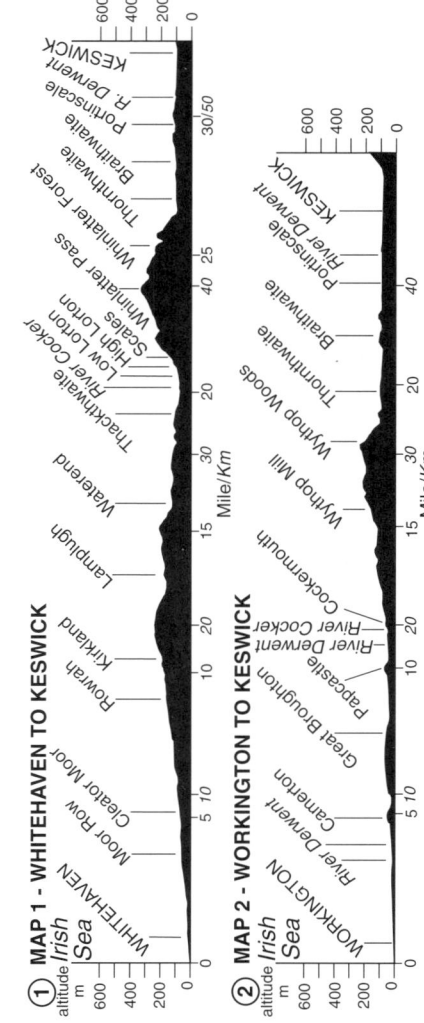

① MAP 1 - WHITEHAVEN TO KESWICK

② MAP 2 - WORKINGTON TO KESWICK

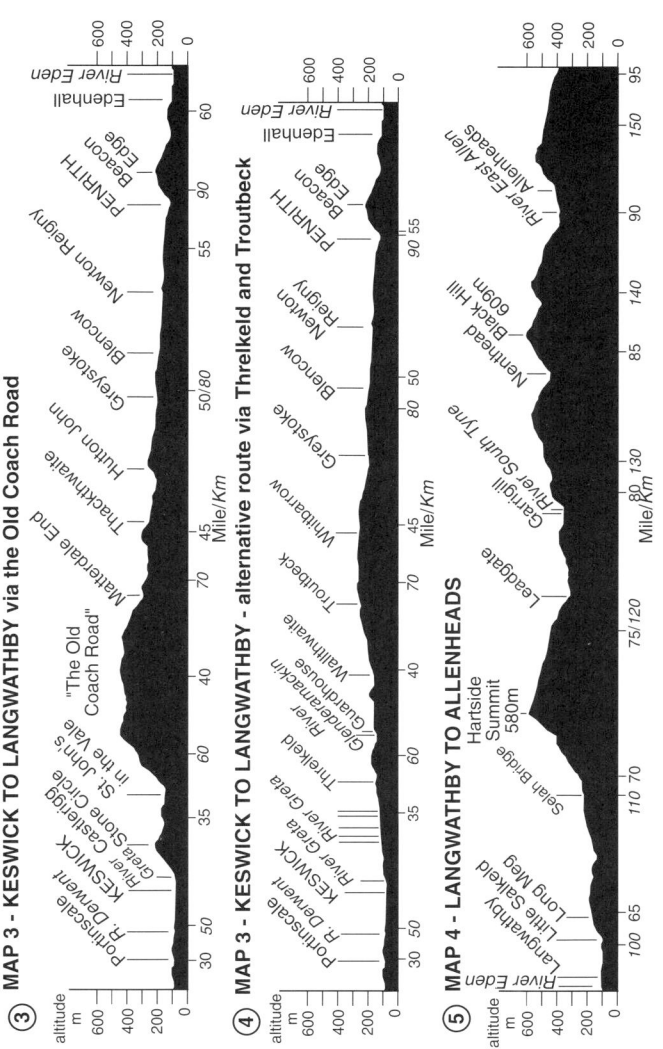

MAP 3 - KESWICK TO LANGWATHBY via the Old Coach Road

③

altitude
m
600
400
200
0

Portinscale · R. Derwent · KESWICK · River Greta · Castlerigg Greta Stone Circle · St. John's in the Vale · "The Old Coach Road" · Mairdale End · Thackthwaite · Hutton John · Greystoke · Blencow · Newton Reigny · PENRITH · Beacon Edge · Edenhall · River Eden

Mile/Km
30   50   35   60   40   45   70   50/80   55   90   60

600
400
200
0

MAP 3 - KESWICK TO LANGWATHBY - alternative route via Threlkeld and Troutbeck

④

altitude
m
600
400
200
0

Portinscale · R. Derwent · KESWICK · River Greta · Threlkeld · River Glenderamackin · Guardhouse · Wallthwaite · Troutbeck · Whitbarrow · Greystoke · Blencow · Newton Reigny · PENRITH · Beacon Edge · Edenhall · River Eden

Mile/Km
30   50   35   60   40   70   45   75   50   80   55   90

600
400
200
0

MAP 4 - LANGWATHBY TO ALLENHEADS

⑤

altitude
m
600
400
200
0

River Eden · Langwathby · Little Salkeld · Long Meg · Selah Bridge · Hartside Summit 580m · Leadgate · Garrigill South Tyne · Nenthead Black Hill 609m · River East Allen Allenheads

Mile/Km
100   65   110   70   75/120   80   130   85   140   90   150   95

600
400
200
0

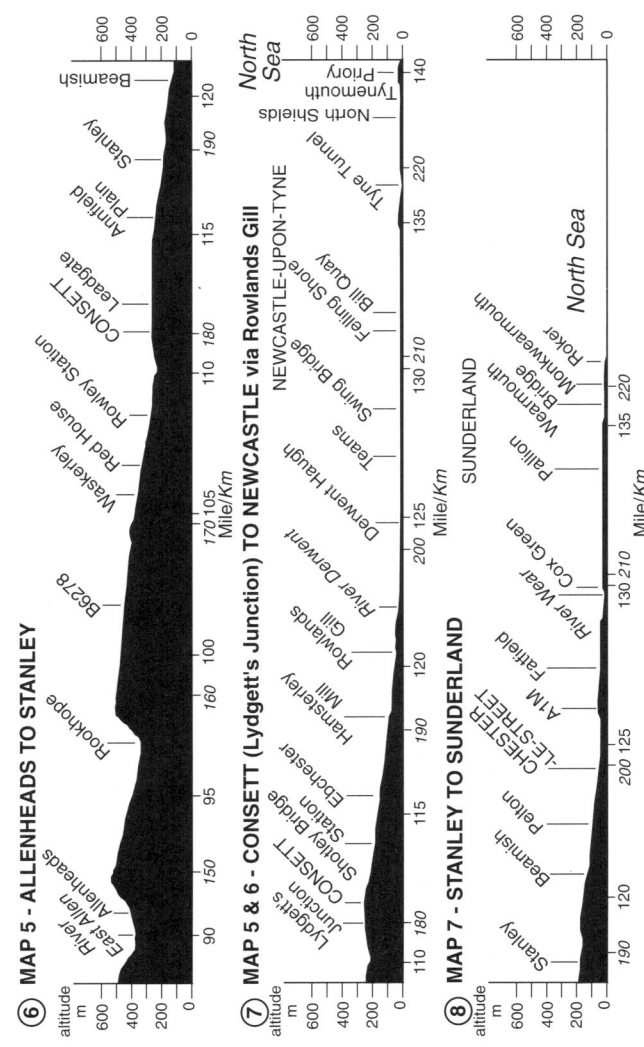

6 MAP 5 - ALLENHEADS TO STANLEY

7 MAP 5 & 6 - CONSETT (Lydgett's Junction) TO NEWCASTLE via Rowlands Gill

NEWCASTLE-UPON-TYNE

8 MAP 7 - STANLEY TO SUNDERLAND

WHITEHAVEN

Whitehaven bay

The town reached its peak of prosperity in the 1740s and 50s with outward trade of coal to Dublin and imports of tobacco from America and rum and sugar from the West Indies. There were early connections with the slave trade together with people settling in America. It was the third busiest port after London and Bristol. The Lowther family laid out the grid pattern

for the Georgian town in the late 1690s. Whitehaven's most notable scientist was William Brownrigg who studied the explosive mine-gas "fire damp". George Washington's grandmother, Mildred Warner Gale, lived in Whitehaven. Don't forget to dip your bike wheel in the Irish Sea! There is a convenient slipway on the harbour front.

The Beacon Visitor Centre

Whitehaven Tourist Information

PLACES OF INTEREST

Michael Moon's, Bookshop & Gallery: largest bookshop
Roper Street in Cumbria, "vast and gloriously
eccentric!"

The Beacon Local maritime and industrial history
within the Harbour Gallery

EATING OUT

Bruno's Restaurant Church St: lively Italian Restaurant
01946 65270

St Nicholas Centre St Nicholas Gardens, Lowther St
01946 64404

The New Expresso 22 Market Place: will do sandwiches
to order. Please phone 01946 591548

CYCLE SHOPS

Kershaw's Cycles 125 Queen Street 01946 590700

Mark Taylor Cycles 5/6 New Street 01946 692252

*C2C Route Features: as you leave Whitehaven you will join
the Whitehaven-Rowrah cycle path which links the sea to the
fells. The railway line was built in the 1850s to carry limestone,
coal and iron; it is now a sculpture trail interpreting the geology
and industrial history of the region. Further down the C2C the
route takes you past the **Whinlatter Visitor Centre**, between
Lorton and Braithwaite. Here you are in the midst of England's
only mountain forest. It contains a wealth of forest habitat
information and is well worth a visit if time and energy allow.
They have a good tea room too.*

Whitehaven

Mrs B. Barwise   Bell House Farm, St. Bees Road,
                                Whitehaven, Cumbria CA28 9UE

Telephone	**01946 692584**
Rooms	2 single + 2 double
B&B	£16.00-£19.00
Packed lunch	£3.50
Distance from C2C	On route Pub nearby

"Newly converted self-contained accommodation on a working family farm. Panoramic views, long-stay parking available. All rooms en-suite. A warm welcome awaits you."

Joyce Bailey   The Cross Georgian Guest House,
                                Sneckyeat Road, Hensingham,
                                Whitehaven, CA28 8JQ

Telephone	**01946 63716**
Rooms	2 double (1 family) + 2 single
B&B	£15.00-£20.00 Packed lunch £2-3.00
Distance from C2C	On route Pub nearby

"A family-run guest-house on the outskirts of Whitehaven. En-suite rooms with Sky TV. Long-term spacious parking is available by arrangement. Lockable storage for bikes."

Mrs Armstrong   Glen Ard Guest House, Inkerman
                                Terrace, Whitehaven, CA28 7TY

Telephone	**01946 692249**
Rooms	2 single + 2 double + 2 twin
B&B	£14.00
Evening meal	£5.00 Packed lunch £3.50
Distance from C2C	$\frac{1}{4}$ mile Pub nearby

"Family-run guest-house with a private car park only $\frac{1}{4}$ mile from the C2C route. Early breakfast available if requested."

13

Whitehaven

Mrs C. M. Oliver   Glenlea House, Glenlea Hill, Lowca,
                         Whitehaven, Cumbria CA28 6PS
Telephone   **01946 693873**   Fax 01946 694350
Rooms   4 single + 8 double
B&B   £17.50-£25.00
Evening meal   £8.50-£10.50 Packed lunch £3.50
Distance from C2C   On route   Pub nearby
*Family-run guest-house. Private car park. Early breakfast
available for those wishing to make the most of the day."*
(See advertisement on page 82.)

Waverley Hotel   Tangier Street, Whitehaven, Cumbria
                         CA28 7UX
Telephone   **01946 694337** Fax   01946 691577
Rooms   10 single + 10 double
B&B   From £22.00 - £35.00
Evening meal   Available   Packed lunch available
Distance from C2C $\frac{1}{4}$ mile   Licensed restaurant
*"300-year-old hotel in centre of historic Whitehaven. All rooms
have colour TV and tea/coffee-making facilities. Very near to
bus and train station."*

T. Todd   The Mansion, Old Woodhouse,
                         Whitehaven, Cumbria CA28 9LN
Telephone   **01946 61860**   Fax 01946 691270
Rooms   3 double + 1 family *(some en-suite)*
B&B   From £11.00
Evening meal   £3.00-£6.00
Distance from C2C   600m   Pub nearby
*"Recently renovated Georgian residence. Sauna, Jacuzzi and
sunbed available. Courtesy pick-up if needed, off-street
parking."*

WORKINGTON

Helena Thompson Museum

Some parts of the town date back to Roman times. Local iron and steel-making helped Workington to expand into a major industrial 18th-century town and port. Famous names linked to the town are Henry Bessemer who introduced his revolutionary steel-making process and Mary Queen of Scots who sheltered in Workington Hall in 1568 on her flight from Scotland. The Hall is now ruined, but is open in summer and is a short distance from the Helena Thompson Museum.

PLACES OF INTEREST

Helena Thompson Museum   Park End Road: a local history gallery together with the famous Clifton dish.

Workington Hall   Apparently haunted by Henry Curwen!

EATING OUT

Impressions   173 Vulcans Lane: Good traditional English food 01900 605446

Super Fish   20 Pow St 01900 604916

CYCLE SHOPS

Traffic Lights Bikes   35 Washington St 01900 603283

New Bike Shop   18-20 Market Place 01900 603337

Workington

Mrs Alice Clark The Boston, 1 St Michael's Road,
        Workington, Cumbria CA14 3EZ
Telephone   **01900 603435**
Rooms   1 family + 2 twin + 1 double/single
B&B   £12.50-£25.00
Distance from C2C 1½ miles Pub nearby
"A small, homely guest-house with a big reputation. A hearty welcome from a friendly family. First-class English breakfast and good home-cooking. Safe parking for bikes and cars."

Mrs Caroline Morven House Hotel, Siddick Road,
 Nelson   Workington, Cumbria CA14 1LE
Telephone/Fax **01900 602118**
Rooms   6 twin/double + 2 single
B&B   £19.50-£24.00
Evening meal   £10.00 Packed lunch £4.00
Distance from C2C On route Pub nearby
ETB 3 Crowns approved. *"A relaxed, informal atmosphere, an ideal stopover for C2C participants near start. Car park and secure cycle storage."* **(See advertisement on page 81.)**

Mrs Hazel Hardy Silverdale, 17 Banklands,
        Workington, Cumbria CA14 3EL
Telephone   **01900 61887**
Rooms   2 double + 2 single
B&B   £13.50-£15.00
Packed lunch   Available on request
Distance from C2C On route Pub nearby
(No smoking in bedrooms please.) "Large Victorian house, quiet location, wash-basins in all bedrooms, bathroom has shower, comfy TV lounge, centrally placed, good parking."